NEW ORLEANS SAINTS · SUPER BOWL CHAMPIONS
XLIV, FEBRUARY 7, 2010
31-17 VERSUS INDIANAPOLIS COLTS

SUPER BOWL CHAMPIONS

NEW ORLEANS SAINTS

AARON FRISCH

CREATIVE EDUCATION

COVER: CORNERBACK TRACY PORTER

PAGE 2: RUNNING BACK REGGIE BUSH BREAKING A TACKLE

RIGHT: FANS CHEERING IN THE LOUISIANA SUPERDOME

Published by Creative Education
P.O. Box 227, Mankato, Minnesota 56002
Creative Education is an imprint of The Creative Company
www.thecreativecompany.us

Design and production by Blue Design (www.bluedes.com)
Art direction by Rita Marshall
Printed by Corporate Graphics in the United States of America

Photographs by Corbis (Bettmann, Tami Chappell/Reuters), Dreamstime (Rosco), Getty Images (Stephen Dunn, Chris Graythen, Otto Greule Jr, Andy Hayt, Jed Jacobsohn, Ronald Martinez, Al Messerschmidt/NFL, Peter Read Miller/Sports Illustrated, Donald Miralle, Mike Powell, Tyrone Turner/ National Geographic, Lou Witt/NFL)

Library of Congress Cataloging-in-Publication Data

Frisch, Aaron.
New Orleans Saints / by Aaron Frisch.
p. cm. — (Super Bowl champions)
Includes index.
Summary: An elementary look at the New Orleans Saints professional football team, including its formation in 1967, most memorable players, Super Bowl championship, and stars of today.
ISBN 978-1-60818-103-2
1. New Orleans Saints (Football team)—History—Juvenile literature. I. Title. II. Series.

GV956.N366F75 2010
796.332'640976335—dc22   2010006568

CPSIA: 040110 PO1141

First Edition
9 8 7 6 5 4 3 2 1

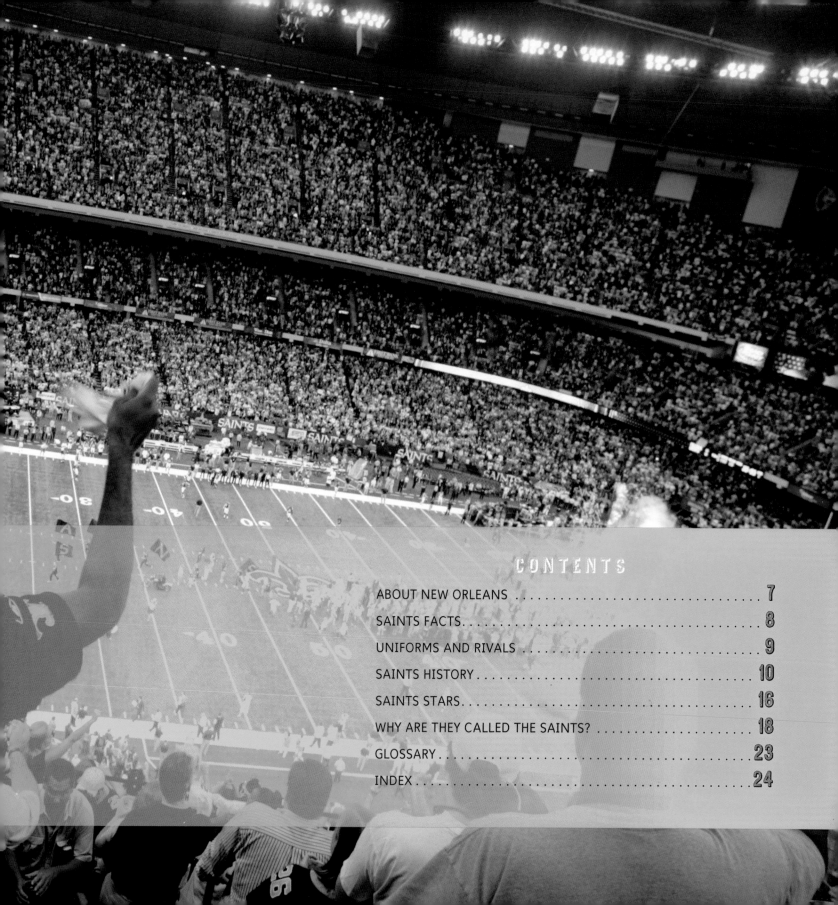

CONTENTS

SUPER BOWL CHAMPIONS

New Orleans is a city in Louisiana. New Orleans is famous for its colorful parades and lively music. It has a stadium called the Louisiana Superdome that is the home of a football team called the Saints.

SAINTS FACTS

First season:
1967

Conference/division:
National Football Conference, South Division

Super Bowl championship:
XLIV, February 7, 2010
31–17 versus Indianapolis Colts

Training camp location:
Metairie, Louisiana

NFL Web site for kids:
http://nflrush.com

8

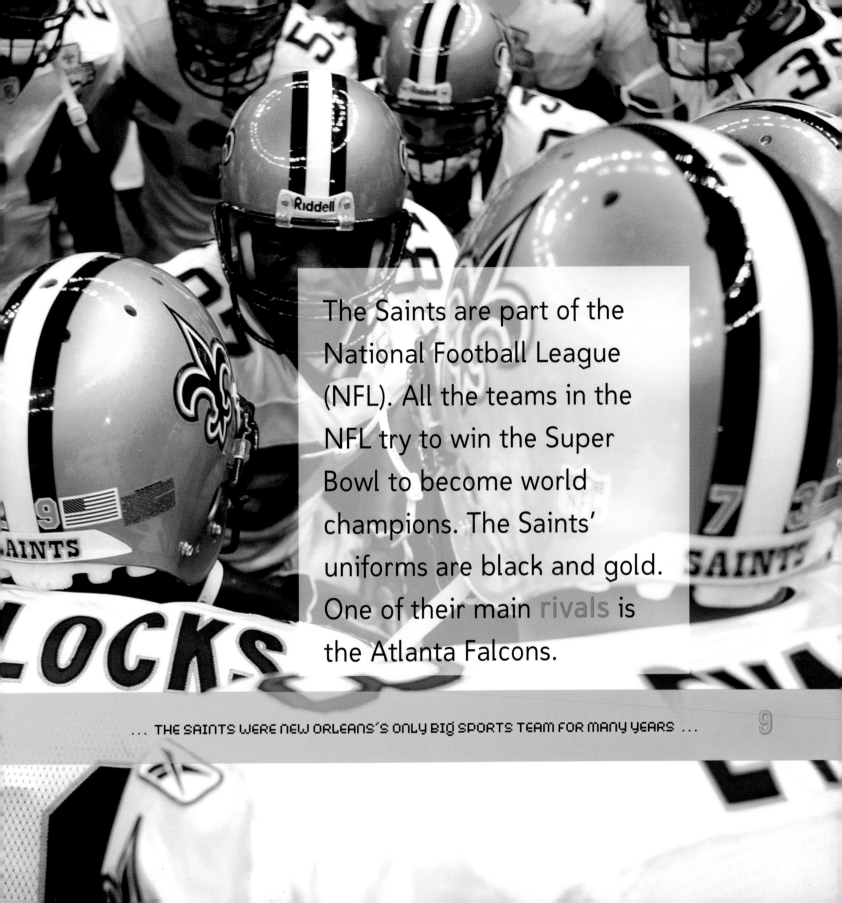

The Saints are part of the
National Football League
(NFL). All the teams in the
NFL try to win the Super
Bowl to become world
champions. The Saints'
uniforms are black and gold.
One of their main rivals is
the Atlanta Falcons.

SUPER BOWL CHAMPIONS

The Saints played their first season in 1967. Tom Dempsey kicked the ball 63 yards for a **field goal** in a 1970 game. That set an NFL **record**! But the Saints were a bad team for a long time.

... TOM DEMPSEY WAS BORN WITHOUT A RIGHT FOOT AND USED A SPECIAL SHOE ...

SUPER BOWL CHAMPIONS

Quarterback Archie Manning was the Saints' biggest star in the 1970s. He played hard every game, but the Saints still lost a lot. New Orleans fans liked to watch fast linebacker Rickey Jackson in the 1980s.

SUPER BOWL CHAMPIONS

The Saints finally started winning after they hired a new coach named Jim Mora. They got to the **playoffs** after the 1990, 1991, and 1992 seasons. But the Saints lost every time.

... RICKEY JACKSON (LEFT) AND ARCHIE MANNING (RIGHT) ...

SUPER BOWL CHAMPIONS

Say It Like This

Brees:
BREEZ

In 2006, New Orleans added quarterback Drew Brees. In 2009, he threw 34 touchdown passes and helped New Orleans get to Super Bowl XLIV (44). The Saints beat the Indianapolis Colts to finally become world champions!

SUPER BOWL CHAMPIONS

Say It Like This

Hebert:

AY-bare

The Saints have had many stars. George Rogers was the NFL's best running back in 1981. He was only a **rookie** then! Quarterback Bobby Hebert liked to throw long passes. Fans called him the "Cajun Cannon."

... BOBBY HEBERT WAS BORN IN LOUISIANA AND BECAME A FAN FAVORITE ...

17

WHY ARE THEY CALLED THE SAINTS?

In the early 1900s, musicians in New Orleans helped create a kind of music called jazz. Jazz is very popular in New Orleans today. One of the most famous jazz songs is called "When the Saints Go Marching In."

Pat Swilling was a fast linebacker in the 1980s and 1990s. He was good at running down quarterbacks. Offensive tackle Willie Roaf was another Saints star. He was a powerful blocker.

... PAT SWILLING WON AN AWARD AS THE NFL'S BEST DEFENSIVE PLAYER IN 1991 ...

... MARQUES COLSTON CAUGHT 70 PASSES FOR NEW ORLEANS IN 2009 ...

The Saints added tall wide receiver Marques Colston in 2006. He scored 33 touchdowns in his first 4 seasons. New Orleans fans hoped that he would help lead the Saints to their second Super Bowl championship!

21
SUPER
BOWL
CHAMPIONS

SUPER BOWL CHAMPIONS

GLOSSARY

field goal — a play where a kicker kicks the ball through the goalposts to score three points

playoffs — games that the best teams play after a season to see who the champion will be

record — something that is the best or most ever

rivals — teams that play extra hard against each other

rookie — a player in his first season

stadium — a large building that has a sports field and many seats for fans

23

SUPER BOWL CHAMPIONS

INDEX